Olivia
all the
light
is you.

73

PRAISE FOR THE BOOK

"To paraphrase Frost, herein are poems that begin in delight and end in a punch to the gut. Behind every turn of phrase, every image, every metaphor, is a story within the story. And each poem is a story, boldly naked, and beautiful in its raw revelation. Falley is a darkly witty and exact wordsmith. These poems aren't simply powerful; they revel in their strength, and demand, deservedly, our attention."

—Dennis Doherty, author of *The Bad Man, Fugitive, Crush Test*

"Falley's love for language and the surgical precision with which she employs her pen is unmatched by her peers. This work is nuanced and subtle yet brutal and unapologetic. I have read these poems over and over and the more I read them, the more they shine."

—Ainsley Burrows, writer and painter

"I love the feminist engine that drives each stanza in *After the Witch Hunt*. The poems are weighted with the kind of strength that can only be born from vulnerability. Personal activism is, after all, the way it starts; we must acknowledge our own dirty roots before we can acquire the power to outgrow them."

—Rachel McKibbens, author of *Pink Elephant*

After the Witch Hunt
a collection of poetry

ঙ

by Megan Falley

Write Bloody Publishing
America's Independent Press

Long Beach, CA

WRITEBLOODY.COM

Falley, Megan.
1ˢᵗ edition.
ISBN: 978-1-935904-62-5

Interior Layout by Lea C. Deschenes
Cover Designed by Anthony Wyborny
Cover Photo by Alison Scarpulla
Author Photo by Jonathan Weiskopf
Proofread by Loulu Losorelli
Edited by Derrick Brown, Miles Walser and Courtney M. Olsen
Type set in Bergamo from www.theleagueofmoveabletype.com

Printed in Tennessee, USA

Write Bloody Publishing
Long Beach, CA
Support Independent Presses
writebloody.com

To contact the author, send an email to writebloody@gmail.com

MADE IN THE USA

*for my mother, who gave me life
more than once.*

for Ana, who left too soon.

AFTER THE WITCH HUNT

After the Witch Hunt

IF YOU REALLY LOVE A WRITER

*"How vain it is to sit down to write
when you have not stood up to live."*
    —Henry David Thoreau

Everyone wants to give a writer the perfect notebook. Over the years I've acquired stacks: one is leather, a rope of Rapunzel's hair braids its spine. Another is tree-friendly, its paper reincarnated from diaries of poets now graying in cubicles. One is small and black as a funeral dress, its pages lined like the hands of a widow. There's even a furry blue one that looks like a shag rug or a monster that would hide beneath it—and I wonder why? For every blown-out candle, every *Mazel Tov*, every turn of the tassel, we are handed what a writer dreads most: blank pages. It's never a notebook we need. If we have a story to tell, an idea carbonating past the brim of us, we will write it on our arms, thighs, any bare meadow of skin. In the absence of pens, we repeat our lines deliriously like the telephone number of a parting stranger until we become the craziest one on the subway. If you really love a writer, fuck her on a coffee table. Find a gravestone of someone who shares her name and take her to it. When her door is plastered with an eviction notice, do not offer your home. Say *I Love You*, then call her the wrong name. If you really love a writer, bury her in all your awful and watch as she scrawls her way out.

During the Week I Thought
I Was Carrying Your Child

I gutted the library, hunting
for what happens when a coyote fucks
a Labrador, if their pup can be trained
to lick the mailman.

Counted all the stairs from my kitchen
to the cellar, sifted through the phonebook
for a friend who loved me enough
to push me down them.

Discovered my mother humming to the garden:
voice fat with water, chrysanthemums
swelling faster from the sound.

During the week I thought
I was carrying your child,
I did not sing.

THE WORST THING I EVER TAUGHT MY GIRL
from my mother's perspective, after Jeanann Verlee

When my daughter came home from school, sorrow shrill
as a recess bell, her story hop-scotching through hiccups
to tell me that Bobby keeps yanking her pigtails
like two ends of a jump rope, calling her
Stupid so often she swears he thinks it's her name—
I cupped her cheeks, shivering like the heart of a snowman,
and said *My baby, my beautiful girl, don't you know? He's trying
to get your attention. It probably means he likes you.*

PENELOPE PUSSYCAT FINALLY SPEAKS
on her career with Warner Bros. and on-set "romance" with Pepé Le Pew

It took fifty years to give me a name.
Half a century of being only his
mon cheri, mademoiselle.

"Penelope Pussycat" they finally stamped me,
a moniker borrowed from a girl corkscrewed
around a pole, dollar bills for panties.
Fitting, they said.

I slinked under a freshly painted ladder
and a white stripe burned into my fur like a scarlet *A*,
meant I was asking for it. That I wanted to always be watched
through binoculars, fancied the trail of drooling kisses
from my paw to collar laid on thick
as his French accent,
that my mad dash from his grasp
meant I liked to be chased, meant yes!—and of course,
they never gave me a voice, just a little French
before small words: *le mew, le purr,*
when bolting from him: *le puff, le pant,*
le gasp!

When Pepé sauntered past, people plugged their noses
with clothespins, buildings wilted around him, paint slid off statues
and kids at home laughed and laughed and spit
out their cereal.

It wasn't because of his stench that I inched off
those cliffs—but how he pretended my refusal was foreplay.
No matter how many times I ran from him, dove
to my cartoon deaths, he was always there
to catch me; The Poster Boy of Romance,
waiting, claws outstretched.

FAMILY

Tell us who did this to you. His
name is not safe in your mouth. Tell
us the shape of his shadow. Your
story. What shade of dusk he wears,
the floorboards he haunts—which
borough? We'd like to meet

the one who turned your body into dangling meat.
Who turned your smile into his
masquerade, who wish-
boned your legs but did not wish? Tell
us who made you hide the silverware—
worry in the night he might slice out your

tongue. Is it true he bit your
tongue 'til your mouth and its story could not meet?
True he marked his height where
his lashings whittled your spine? His
hands—is it true he never used them? Tell
us how he made the scars then. Which

scar is shaped most like a muzzle? Which
injury rendered you so quiet? You're
scared now, thinking about his laughter—we can tell.
His laughter like an army of hornets, the meat
of your every nightmare. Everyone knows *his*
story, the lion who *baaahs* like a lamb. Where

is the last place he'd ever hide? Think. Where?
We want to know what time he leaves which
bar. Notice our ears—they are larger than his.
The better to hear you with, darling. Your
story, we want it, the marrow and the meat
of it. And if it hurts to tell

we have brought the pliers, tell!
Or *we'll* open your lips. The Guest of Honor must know where
the barbeque is. We are already sharpening our skewers to meet
your body. As you roast above we will shout your many names: *Witch,*
Whore. Bitch. Cunt. Liar. Cheat. Liar. You're
a liar. Burn, liar. Silly girl, our love was only ever *his.*

Tell us where to find him so we can ask how
he likes his meat, which of your eyes he
would prefer as the jewel in his crown.

The Honest House

In an effort not to crawl back to you,
I crossed the 2 train off my subway map
in blue ink, called it a river, sold our canoe.

Swept the soot from the chimney into a vase,
scattered it over our favorite spots in Manhattan.
Husband, I pretended they were your ashes.

Spoke your name in past tense. Still,
when we found ourselves in the same bar, I phoned a mystic,
told her I was seeing ghosts.

When you confessed your mistress—her red hair,
her scars, how you learned them from up-close,
from inside out—you were no longer the man I married
but a dead deer in the center of our swimming pool.

Our dog has always considered you a burglar, knew to spit bark bite
before I did. Once, while you were sleeping, I stitched her electric fence
through your skin. I wear her shock collar on nights I go out drinking,
on days I can't find a reason to stay away from you
even though you have left so many behind.

I've watched you with other women:
the way you hand fruit to the supermarket clerk,
how your eyebrow lifts for anyone with fake nails.
Your favorite party story is how you once, publicly,
pleasured a girl with your band mate's drumstick.
(It's no wonder we don't love the same music.)

On our first date, I bought a dress from a woman
in Brooklyn so I could stay with you one more day.
Yesterday I threw your clothes from our roof
knowing they would have fallen faster
had there been a body in them.

When I found a picture of your ex-lover's tits
used as a bookmark, I began opening every novel upside down
like a teenager shakes birthday cards waiting for cash to fall out.
This explains my love for fiction:
> we were never married.
> The dog is not *ours*.

While washing the dishes, I watch from the window as the children
we never had drown in the piss-filled pool.
I have never tried to save them.
I invented that pool, this sink.

Did you know that the metronome inside of us quickens when telling a lie?
I want to live in an honest house
where the motion detector is so sharp
it knows when my thoughts leave the room.

I want a clap on lamp that works as a polygraph;
when you swear you still love me, the lights flicker.

ADAM'S APPLE PIE
a recipe

Ingredients:

- 1 ½ cups sugar.
- 2 hands (his) marinated overnight inside the woman you caught
  him with.
- His eye (the wandering one) al dente.
- The time he said no one one would ever love you as much as he
  did, pulverized into a teaspoon of pulp.
- A bouillon cube of their sweat.
- The apple, plucked from his throat, then cored.
- His heart (if it is not a myth) browned over the rotisserie.

Best enjoyed without utensil, just claw and gorge.

Prep: As long as it takes.
Cook: Until it does not burn.
Serves: Him. Right.

THE POET'S FATHER
after Molly Giles

The oldest man at the poetry reading sits alone and stares at his hands: working hands that smell like newspaper, hands that know shaving cream is the best way to soften a catcher's mitt, large hands with a ring finger that has been claimed by three wives, and when a woman takes the stage several moments pass before he realizes it's his daughter; she's a whole foot taller and has breasts now which he is certain were not there before and he watches her, as if for the first time, telling a room full of people about the men she's fucked, the drugs she's tasted, a comment he made fifteen years ago that she never forgot and never forgave, and when she leaves the stage he watches as the boys' eyes follow her, hair: long and let down—he was expecting pigtails—and she asks *Daddy, can I buy you a drink?* while the bartender pours her favorite without asking, smooches both cheeks, and after the long drive from Manhattan to suburbia he pulls into his garage, kisses his new wife and doesn't mention the poems or the woman who read them but how the ride home felt like it passed in a blink.

FIELD TRIP

With our peanut butter and jellies ripening
in our brown paper lunches, complete with napkin notes
from mom (if you were loved)—
my fourth grade class, all coveting a seat
beside the impeccable Ashley Rose,
single-filed onto the school bus.
We buzzed from 99 bottles of beer
on the wall, joy-drunk like prisoners
sprung from our classroom cells.
We were headed to Safety Town: a miniature city
built to teach nine-year-olds the meaning
of yield signs, how to cross a street without dying,
the significance of traffic lights
changing like autumn leaves.
Each student was paired with a bicycle,
introduced to a new language of arm movements
indicating *right turn, left turn, stop.*
One by one I watched
my classmates pedal away like ducklings
first learning to explore, leaving me—
the only fourth grader in the entire world
who never learned to ride a bike.
The crossing guard fastened the helmet strap
under my chin, guided my fingers to imaginary handlebars,
complimented my invisible blue bicycle's horn and basket.
Friends whizzed by as if propelled by a secret
everyone knew but me.
When I came home, I stole
my brother's two-wheeler, carried it
out into the yard like an animal
I intended to slaughter, determined
to ride off all the way into adolescence
where the bright red humiliation of the day
faded out like distant taillights.
And I rode and rode
and rode and rode until I broke
my own arm.

To the Women Competing on E! Entertainment's Hit Reality Television Show, "Bridalplasty":

Whoever loved you, loved *you*. Loved your scars and their legends, loved each vagabond hair. The first time he caught you—lit up by the bright light of a midnight refrigerator, sneaking cookie dough into your mouth—he knew he would marry you. While you slept he called his mother to tell her, skated his finger down the bend in your nose and imagined it on a future daughter's face. If he were a surgeon, he would chisel away at his patients until the whole world looked just like you. If he were a painter, there would be one million of your eyes opening all over this gritty metropolis. To him, you are perfect. But he is a simple man and the only way he knows how to tell you this is by turning on the lights when you make love—and you turn them right off.

When you were little, your mother would hoist up her blouse and blame your birth for her stomach, how it hung like wet linen. In her fairytales, gravity always played the villain. You used to dream that you could take your tummy to the butcher shop and he would carve you thin with a deli slicer; so when you told your fiancée you would be competing against other brides-to-be for a Hollywood doctor to correct the lazy hand of God—he did not say no. He had not seen you smile this wide since mono robbed the childbearing from your hips. He remembered how the pounds crawled back on like a relapse of cancer, a ghost you thought you could kill.

On the show they snip out freckles he had names for, plump your lips until they feel like someone else's kiss. Your nipples sit on a cold tray table while a doctor stuffs you like a Thanksgiving bird. You ignore the warnings that you will never have sensation in your breasts again. The sensation is installing a mirror on your ceiling, a teenage boy who whistles at you in a swimsuit.

You already have the one that loves you. The one who saw the way your stomach hung over your pants and said *yes, take, want*. The one who loved your smaller breast and took it in his mouth first every time.

What will you tell your five-year-old daughter when she cannot find her face in yours? Or says, "Mommy, when I grow up, I want to be a centerfold"? When you discover the first Tupperware of vomit stuffed in the back of her closet?

When you win your dream wedding, America will watch from their living rooms as you float toward your groom in your perfect new body upholstered in your perfect new dress, and he'll lift your perfect veil and see—the wrong woman. He'll look around the room for the culprit, for whoever replaced his bride with a doll, the sparkle in her eye just painted on.

FAT GIRL

after Angel Nafis, after Terrance Hayes

Fat girl fat jokes.
Fat girl skinny friends.
Fat girl stand next to fatter people to look thin.
Fat girl fat camp for five years.
Fat girl lost two pounds and *you* didn't notice.
Fat girl love your garlic breath.
Fat girl vegan.
Fat girl but red velvet cupcake tastes so delicious.
Fat girl pretty face.
Fat girl Dean's List.
Fat girl want fries with that.
Fat girl *don't* touch her stomach.
Fat girl turn the lights off.
Fat girl keep her t-shirt on.
Fat girl not pregnant.
Fat girl food baby.
Fat girl named her dog Taco.
Fat girl love her skinny mirror.
Fat girl bad bulimic.
Fat girl binge and no purge.
Fat girl can't even throw up right.
Fat girl unbutton her pants at dinner.
Fat girl heard "nothing tastes as good as being thin feels."
Fat girl certain spicy crunchy tuna rolls taste better than being thin feels.
Fat girl threw out her scale.
Fat girl "you are what you eat."
Fat girl Double Stuf Oreos.
Fat girl got her father's genes.
Fat girl's brother didn't.
Fat girl's friends come over to stare at her brother's chiseled
        abdominals and ignore
Fat girl don't hate her body.
Fat girl hate the world.
Fat girl fat mouth.
Fat girl fatter fist.
Fat girl fuck you.

Fat girl heart so fat it needs its own zip code.
Fat girl heart so fat it uses the equator as its belt.
Fat girl seafood diet.
Fat girl see food, fat girl eat it.
Fat girl heard *all* the jokes.
Fat girl finish the punch line before you do.
Fat girl cry in private.
Fat girl thick skin.
Fat girl dance anyway.
Fat girl shirt off.
Fat girl lights on.
Fat girl
lights
on.

GRETEL GROWS UP
from my mother's perspective

My brother Billy was still young enough to be proud.
To him, living in the back of my parent's candy store
in 1964's shanty Brooklyn was like waking up
in an Easter basket.

It didn't matter that we could hardly afford the lint
in our pockets, that we couldn't cuddle a cockroach the way we might
a dog—Coca-Cola signs became his nightlight, the pesky ring
of an opening cash register: his morning alarm,
the floor mattresses of our shared bedroom: a three-year slumber party.

He would present our new home to friends like the ringmaster
of our ridiculous circus, convinced he had won
The Golden Ticket.

When kids from school stopped in, I'd sneak out
the back door or sit on the customer's side
of the counter like I was only visiting.

Years later when my own privileged daughter would beg
to know what my favorite treat in the store was,
her eyes: pinwheel lollipops; lips: Swedish Fish jumping
to the bait, expecting my head to tilt back like a Pez dispenser,
presenting her with a small, sweet brick,

I told her my favorite part of the candy store
was the sour pickles from the deli next door,
dripping with vinegar.

THE PINK RIBBON PARADE
for the women of Nassau County from 1994-1997

When the Long Island tap water sunk its venom
into the neighborhood women, teenage boys mowed their lawns
for free, inquired how the ladies were *feeling* with smiles
straight and white as hospital beds.

I watched from my school bus as the housewives bled
from their brick homes, heads cloaked with imported silk.
Small pink ribbons pinned to their blouses marked a secret
society, a glamour limited to mothers
of my friends.

The town held parties in their honor,
began walking marathons for these women—
but I couldn't even get my father to carry me
on his shoulders anymore.

When the first unraveled
her kerchief I was afraid of her head: bald as a cello.
Remembered fishing my hair from the toilet bowl
after I hacked my own bangs, the Barbie dolls
I ruined with crew cuts, never
played with again.

But this was *not so bad*, they told me.
A straight-haired lady might suddenly sprout spirals—
as if God were holding her ponytail and a scissor
the way mom curled ribbons
on Christmas presents.

When I first saw a collection of wigs
on decapitated mannequins, I loved them,
like picket fences painted at the tip.
Each morning a chance to be someone new:

> Blonde as a sunflower.
> Red as a mermaid on fire.

Cancer was like a television makeover show.
It was Oprah glittering on your doorstep
with a four-foot check, a brand new wardrobe.
I stared in the mirror and tugged
at my limp brown pigtails, waiting
for my turn.

Pendulum

I met your brother once.
His fifteen-year-old face lit up
the party like a fishbowl of fireflies hung
from the rafters.

The frat boys trained him
to jab a knife into the side
of a beer can, pull the tab
and *shotgun*.

Us girls showed him
how to blow halos
of smoke.

I taught him the way to sink
a ball in beer pong. With every shot,
he high-fived the ceiling like he was testing
if the beams were sturdy.

From us he learned adulthood
was best enjoyed blacked out
and forgotten by dawn,
our blotto heartbeats buzzing
like hotline busy signals.

In the morning he thought he could resurrect
the simplicity of childhood by turning
into a tire swing.

Was his favorite part of the Wizard of Oz
not the Lion finding courage,
the Tin Man finding heart?
But the extra in the background
drooping like a necktie?

When your mother reached up
into his pockets, digging for answers,
all she found was a family
of paperclips: unlinked.

I wonder what the hurry was to die.
When he turned himself into a pendulum,
what became of time?

WHAT THE HOUR HAND SAID
TO THE MINUTE HAND

At 6:32 a.m. you lay your tired body on mine before peeling off like
the slowest Band-Aid.
At 7:38 you sprint home and make instant coffee.
At 8:43 we finally drink it, cold. I finish your leftover half.
By 9:49 you are already breathless. I live for every time we overlap.
When 10:54 comes I spend the entire minute convincing you to stay.
You never do.
By noon I put my hands on your shoulders and say, "Baby, you're
getting thin. All this running in circles and barely sitting down to eat."
At 1:05 you tell me that while you were gone 15,300 babies were born.
At 2:10 you don't say a word, just come and kiss me for sixty seconds
straight.
At 3:16 I read aloud from *The Giving Tree*. It's your favorite book
because you've never heard how it ends.
At 4:21 I tell myself *catch her!* but it's like I'm stuck in a spill of syrup.
At 5:27 I hear the ticking. I count your heartbeat like seconds
between thunderclaps.
At 6:32 I see you in the distance, each moment a tease until you
drape over me. We always love quick and you never let me hold you.
I dream of drinking you through a straw.
At 7:38 you watch my beard grow 0.00027 of an inch.
At 8:43 we do not speak. Too many people have died since we last met.
By 9:49 we get selfish, pray for the apocalypse, anything to stop the
cruel bully of time.
At 10:54 you'll apologize sixty times because it will always be like this.
By midnight I have already fallen asleep. It's exhausting loving
someone who is constantly running away.

THE MOST BEAUTIFUL WORD
IN THE ENGLISH DICTIONARY

"stay."

No Name

from my mother's perspective

"If you lose a spouse, you're called a widow, or a widower. If you're a child and you lose your parents, then you're an orphan. But what's the word to describe a parent who loses a child? I guess that's just too fucking awful to even have a name."
—Brenda Chenowith, *Six Feet Under*

1.
His sister found the pills—
some sixth sense siblings have, a feeling
like drowning. She's a good girl, sad. I worry
she's raised herself. I love her no less
but every parent runs first
to the child that's bleeding.

All this time I've kept a lock
of his baby blonde hair, use it as a bookmark.
Haven't made his bed since he left
so that everyday looks like he's just woken up.

I refuse to paint over the height marks
I penciled on the garage, stacked like scars
up a forearm. I wish he was still small
as the first gash.

We haven't flushed his sixty-eight Vicodin.
Maybe he will come back for them. Maybe
they will take us to where he goes
when his eyes fog over like that,
to the place he loves more
than his family.

Today I hung a painting of a lotus flower
in front of the hole in the wall but I won't
plaster over it; this replica of his fist
is the closest thing I have
to his hands.

2.
When her husband's head
was shot off, Jackie Kennedy scrambled
to collect the puzzle of his scalp
as if having all the pieces might revive him.
If you love someone, no part of them
is revolting. Every bloody bit: beautiful.

BOY SCOUT

He smelled like sleigh rides.
Locked my cell phone in the glove box, sprinted
up the mountain like a stag dodging an arrow. I was slower,
he was teaching me to trust my own ankles.

At the summit we read his dead father's poetry
from a dusty binder. He had never shown anyone before.
It was like someone handing back your virginity
as if it had just been out late wandering on the back of a milk carton.

In his pocket lived a box of strike-anywhere matches.
I lifted up his shirt and sparked one down his stomach.
Together our hands were thatched roofs,
our sex was a wood-burning stove.

That night we spotted a black bear for the first time.
He called it an omen, a symbol of our love. It became an obsession.
While he slept, I drew a bear on his torso, fried his eggs
in the shape of two ears and a snout, cherry tomatoes for the eyes.
At night I'd curl into him like a cub.

Our love ended. I never understood how he could fit his life
into a knapsack. He couldn't comprehend why I was desperate
to pour mine into poems.

A year later he calls and cannot wait to tell me he saw
a black bear again—but this time it was too late. He didn't see it
in the road. The grille of his pick-up found it first. Its coarse fur
pecked the windshield like hard rain. He pulled over.
Lugged its tire-tracked body to the side of the road. Unzipped it
with his pocketknife. Slid the muscle from its skin
like a gentleman helps his lady remove her fur coat.
Built a fire with his two good hands. Ate for days.

For him, I know this is efficiency,
not betrayal. A tale of survival without metaphor.
He doesn't know what I hear: that it is our love
he is running over again and again, picking the shreds of us
from his teeth, wiping the last of me clean from his lips.

A boy scout wastes nothing.

Friday Night Between 2ND Avenue and Herald Square

the union square robot man is actually *in* this subway car but his
movements are human now and i'm wishing he'd washed the silver
paint off his body before coming here 'cause its like seeing the elastic
holding up a shopping mall santa's beard but he gives a wink as i pull
out my notebook or maybe it was meant for the girl next to me who
is still beautiful despite vomiting in her pocketbook and passing out
on my shoulder like she knows me and totally oblivious to the grown-
ass woman across from us with the hello kitty tattoos who keeps
calling me *cunt nugget* like it's a compliment while the pinstriped man
looks up from his cell phone for the first time just to see if drunk girl
has lost a tit but i'm not one to judge 'cause i only look up from my
notebook for an extra detail to drape over a poem like tinsel while a
beggar sings in the subway car like it's her shower even though it's
clear she hasn't showered this season as passengers throw change at her
like breadcrumbs to a dirty city pigeon and *shit* she caught me staring
don't look crazy in the face no look at the child with six pink balloons
pop one pops and everyone's eyes scurry around the train car searching
for the bullet and waiting for their shirt to soak through with blood.

This Poem Came Quick

He likes when I handcuff us together
but not when I swallow the key.

I tell him I want to savor
his nipples like after dinner mints

and this makes him erect
as the Chrysler Building.

When I explain this means I'll need to keep
his nipples in my desk drawer, he hides

the razors. He likes when I tie him up
but not when I leave him

there for days, until I can count
all 206 of his bones, give them

new names. He is thin as a war
prisoner, I become his wet nurse.

He hallucinates that his bedroom
is an ocean. I shimmy through

his fingers, he claws away
trying to give me new gills.

My fin tickles, he drops me,
he has caught a mermaid,

spends the next few minutes
figuring out how to give me legs

just so he can part them. He parts them
with his tongue. His tongue is a tentacle.

He likes when I pull his hair
but not when I rip it clear off his head,

dress the locks in children's clothes,
put them to sleep in beds made of matchboxes.

I want bald spots, want whole clumps
gone, he can be pretty

for no other woman,
must look like he has a disease

you can catch
through eye contact.

And in the throes of this lion–
like passion, this head bent

and howl, this sweat that belongs
to neither in particular

he begs me to fuck
him until he dies

so I do.

Bringing Over the Jell-O Mold

Thinking of me
while inside another woman
must feel like sitting in the new neighbor's dining room,
saying you preferred the people who lived there
before.

Haikus Found on the (One) Nightstand

I know we haven't
spoken about that thing we
did with our bodies.

If it's okay with
you, be quiet as slipping
through morning's window.

When I ring up your
groceries, pretend I have
not scanned your torso,

that I never spent
the night learning exactly
how much you are worth.

SAMOA

A boy named after a bird opened my mouth with his unclean fingers, stuck a small square of paper rocking the iconic Rolling Stones logo directly on my tongue. "See you later," he said. It was my first time.

I didn't want the German men to trip with us girls, they were flirtatious and there were enough foreign things in our bodies, but when they floated over—pupils eclipsing their irises—we knew we were in this together, an army of Wild Things, ready for the Technicolor ocean to charm our hair into crowns of seaweed, for the salt to smoke us like fish, for the spongy fingers of coral to pull us into the vault of earth. Here we were, splashing in the aquamarine puddle of a Goddess' belly button. I floated on my back as Chloe led me through the water. She was the latest brand of dinosaur and I her pet human.

It didn't matter that the night before I slept with an arm outside of the mosquito net and today my elbow was a blistering grapefruit, or that I had spent my rent money on this particular escape—just that no one wanted to make us noodles and we were starving, that we were sure the Germans were alligators wearing skin suits and swim trunks, that the sun was going to come down and we weren't.

The outdoor shower was a jungle we couldn't enter alone. Stepping out of our bikini bottoms and untying each other's tops, the three of us passed the soap back and forth like a slippery fish. Vivian was shaved, like me, but Chloe had a bush the size of 1971 and I could see the pale memory of their bathing suits, the rest of our skin pink and raw like the innards of an invented fruit. I knew then, even more magnificent than this private island where the palm trees would knot in an orgy of limbs, more than the way the moon would unleash its glowing braid of silvery hair down the midnight ocean's back, even more than how the sun would wake the sky in some faraway hour, a citrus slit that would swell into a slice, a melon, even more magnificent

were women.

THE FIRST (NOEL)

Noel was the reason boys had lockers—
not to hold textbooks, but to hang her senior picture.
Her infectious Brooklyn accent was singlehandedly responsible
for the influx of twentysomethings in that borough.
Noel's legs were the reason girls like me
were gung-ho for gym class indoor soccer.

For reasons I will never know, I was chosen.
Noel was the messiah that saved me
from the hell of my sophomore year.

During 6th period she would take me
for a ride, her hand dominating the clutch, Britney Spears
singing through the subwoofers and my entire grade wondering
why this beautiful senior picked me to ride shotgun.
I became cool-by-proxy, the potato sack
a celebrity wears one time and turns it famous.
Had she wanted, Noel could make a skin rash trendy.

When she refused to pledge allegiance
to the flag, I took my hand off my heart.
When she came to school on Halloween without costume,
I washed the wicked-witch green from my face
in the girl's bathroom, its leftover stain
coloring me with putrid envy.

I would have never guessed that Noel was a Jehovah's Witness
(for God's sake, her name meant Christmas!).
But she spoke of her religion like a telemarketer
who only calls when you are lonely, selling the one
thing you really need.

When she invited me, a half-Jew
who'd lost God in the same fire as the tooth fairy,
to a private bible study, I said *Amen*.
Spent afternoons memorizing the first ten books of the Scriptures
because that made her eyes come alive like two animals

I was thankful Noah made room for on his arc.
When she said we would get "closer to God,"
I heard the Nine Inch Nails song, not the church choir.

The lessons stopped when there were things I couldn't understand:
why it was an abomination for a man to lay next to another man
when a few passages earlier she'd highlighted, "God is Love."
Noel got married before she could legally drink at her wedding. I was
    not invited.

I know she doesn't have a birthday to be called on, and what would I
    even say?
That in my language, Christmas means to unwrap?
That while her beliefs forbid her to take another's blood,
there was a time I would have offered mine?
That I might be the only person in the world
who gets a little excited at the sound of an unexpected doorbell?—
The only girl who prays
it just might be
a witness.

THE ATHEIST

The first time we made love I realized why
I never prayed. One human can only say
Oh God so many times.

Upon Realizing That the "I" Section of My iPod Is a Perfect Alphabetical Summation of My Love Life
a found poem

I am a rock.
I am in love with you.
I am the walrus.

I and I.
I believe love will find a way.

I cried for you.
I did it my way.
I didn't understand.
I don't believe you.
I don't give a fuck.
I don't mean it.
I don't want to die in a hospital.
I don't want to get over you.
I don't want to spoil the party.

I fall apart.
I feel fine.
I feel it all.
I feel just like a child.
I feel like dying.

I felt your shape.
I forgot to remember to forget.

I get around.
I got mine.
I got to find my baby.
I gotta right to sing the blues.
I heard it through the grapevine.
I just don't think I'll ever get over you.

I kissed a drunk girl.
I know.
I know you know.
I left my wallet in El Segundo.
I love college.

I never loved a man (the way that I love you).
I never loved you anyway.
I shall be released.

I think I need a new heart.

I threw it all away.
I used to love her.
I used to love him.
I want it all.

I want to hold your hand.
I want to know your plans.
I want you.
I want you to want me.

I will follow you into the dark.
I will possess your heart.

I'll be that girl.
I'll be your friend.
I'll get by.

I'm a cuckoo.
I'm a lady.
I'm a loser.
I'm a slave 4 U.
I'm a thug.
I'm amazed.
I'm good at being bad.
I'm good, I'm gone.
I'm like a bird.
I'm lonely (but I ain't that lonely yet).

I'm not a girl, not yet a woman.
I'm not going anywhere tonight.
I'm not gonna teach your boyfriend how to dance with you.

I'm sensitive.
I'm shady.
I'm so tired.
I'm sticking with you.
I'm with you.
I've been eating (for you).

I've got a feeling.
I've got to see you again.
I've just seen a face.
I've underestimated my charm (again).

If winter ends.
If you had my love.
If you love somebody, set them free.
If you want to sing out, sing out!

In case we die (In da club/In the airplane over the sea/In the backseat/
In the car/In the dark/In the devil's territory/In the morning before
work/In this hole/In this home on ice/In this lonely town/Incomplete
and insecure)—Is this love?

It could be sweet.
It makes no difference.
It won't be long.
It's a disaster.
It's a fire.
It's all been done.
It's all gonna break.

It's all over now, baby blue.

WE HAD NO CHILDREN

When our hamster Gus died
in a disfiguring accident on the wheel,

I used a baby tooth for a tombstone.
Too small to fit his whole name,
I left off the "G,"

buried "us" in the backyard.
Forecast says: snow—everywhere.
Like a shroud.

HARRY HARLOW RESURRECTS
TO REMIND ME I AM INDEED ALONE

When I first read about his Rhesus Monkey experiment—how when ripped from their mothers and given two options: a ragdoll that provided no nourishment except the softness of a mama or a hard wire torso pinned with a nipple of milk, and how the monkeys clung hungry to the body that felt most like a hug—I ran to the kitchen, devoured six clementines undressed with no tenderness, wild salmon caught in an aluminum can, linguini pulled from its boiling bath before supple, hummus nestled in a bed of lettuce, all washed down with a quart of chocolate soy milk and celebrated the comfort, the spills and sauces mixing on my chin and shirt like some haphazard potluck and no one to judge me! No one to tell me to shave my armpits or do Pilates or let me shiver on the other end of the shower while they rinse their shampoo, no need to compromise anything—just me, my stocked fridge, my empty house where I can turn the music up as loud as I want! And no one will step on my feet when I dance by myself and I got a new flat-screen television: each year's model thinning like the actresses who live inside it and no one's gonna change this channel. No one's gonna hog these blankets. No one's gonna keep me awake with the stupid sounds of their dreaming or say *God Bless You* and I can buuuuuuuuuuuuuuuurp "The Star-Spangled Banner" and talk to any of my one thousand five-hundred and ninety-four friends on my little machine all night while they sit home talking to me on their little machines all night and I got a whole list of names in this phonebook that I'm not close enough with to just call, and suddenly everything— the very place I sit. This ridiculous thread count. This goose down. This Tempur-Pedic pillow: the only thing that remembers my shape— hardens. Turns to wire.

Rain

The commercial begins with a woman on a swing set.
A small blue cloud hovers over her head as if just hatched
and she was the first thing it saw.

A calm, medicated voice narrates:
*"It follows you wherever you go. It's a cloud of depression and although
you've been on an antidepressant for at least six weeks, you're frustrated that
your depressive symptoms are still with you. Seroquel XR, when added to an
antidepressant, is approved for the treatment of major depressive disorder."*

Around this point in the commercial
I begin to wonder why my antidepressants need antidepressants,
why my little happy pills need little happy pill friends
to push them to their fullest potential
and achieve their greatest purpose.

Slowly, the woman regains her ability to smile
at her kid's soccer game, pet her dog, chop
a carrot, and the cloud trails off
as if it found another head to hover over.

The voice returns, listing the side effects
as if they were a bedtime story:

*"Call your doctor if you have fever, stiff muscles and confusion as these can
be signs of a life-threatening reaction, or if you have uncontrollable muscle
movements as these can become permanent. High blood pressure has also been
reported with Seroquel XR and in extreme cases can lead to coma, or death.
Other risks include decrease in white blood cells (which can be fatal), seizures,
increased cholesterol, weight gain, dizziness on standing, drowsiness, impaired
judgment, long-lasting painful erections and trouble swallowing. Call your
doctor if you experience any changes in mood, behavior, or thoughts of suicide."*

Around this point I begin wondering—if I'm trying
not to kill myself, why is a side-effect of this drug *wanting*
to kill myself?

But the woman in the commercial—in all likelihood
now thirty pounds heavier and also in a coma,
unable to operate heavy machinery or swallow
her boyfriend's long-lasting painful erection
would probably be *more* depressed with these symptoms
if she wasn't such a fucking zombie … but at least that damn cloud is gone!
And I want to know if she misses it.

Because I'm thinking—give me that cloud.
Give me these evenings where I do nothing but sit
in a bloodless bubble bath until my skin prunes
like that of an old woman
ready to die.

Give me these days where I'd rather watch my dog shit
on the carpet than take either of our asses outside.

Give me *The Bell Jar*, how Plath turns suicide
into a freshly baked scent that pulls you
to its oven.

Give me that stupid, reliable cloud
because it might be the only thing
that never leaves.

Because being *only* happy
is like having just one crayon—
even if it's the prettiest crayon,
it sure gets boring.

Give me that cloud.
Give me this ache that lets me know
I'm alive.

Only-Child Practice

When we hear my brother's voice
on the answering machine, we don't want
to lower the television.

The family on screen demands
our immediate attention.
They have spent more time in our living room
than he has all year.

We figure he is calling to ask if we have room
in our washer and dryer, or mail sent to him
by people who think he still lives
here.

We know it is not Mother's Day,
or either of our birthdays, because today
he called.

But his voice sounds dimmer, mutters
the name of a hospital, something about a strip club,
a frat brother, a car curling around a telephone pole
like an exotic dancer, a broken hand, a tooth
cut clear through a chin.

We hope this is the last almost-death,
the awkward hospital gown
that finally makes recklessness un-cool.

I have never loved him more than I do when he needs me
to cut his toast, when he struggles to open a butter packet
with his left hand.

He tosses me a dollar to fetch him something
from the vending machine. I return to his side
with a bottle of cola, proud as a housecat:
a trophy bird in her jaw.

Coconut Verbena

My father gets discounted tickets for being a senior citizen at Six Flags Great Adventure. The theme park assumes, because of his age, he will skip out on all the rides and hold the colas. My father is always the oldest person in line for every single coaster. He will wait the extra hour for a seat in the last row, for the car that makes the rider feel closest to death.

There is a repertoire of games we no longer play: "Who Can Fall Asleep First"—a contest I never found out the winner of, the "Cold Feet Game"—where I'd place my popsicle toes on his space heater calves, and "Snow White"—where he would bring me a juicy red apple and a tiny bite was the only way I'd fall asleep. In the morning it was "Sleeping Beauty"—a forehead kiss from him was the only way I'd wake.

Once I ran into the Green Acres Mall fountain to collect the pennies at the bottom. He tried using his voice as fishing line, but eventually had to follow in after, pretending to be mad until the laughter found us—soaked and ridiculous in the elevator.

Before I could read, I'd crack open the fat legs of a fortune cookie and ask him what they said: "Megan is the most beautiful girl in the world." Every time.

He would always come home with shopping bags full of different scented shampoos and tell me to close my eyes. He'd pop open their heads and I'd guess their flavors. I imagine him walking through fluorescent-lit stores he needed nothing from just to play this game with me, picture him smirking at scents he knew would stump me: Coconut Verbena, Key Lime Pie. I can see the perplexed convenience store clerk selling countless bottles of hair product to a very bald man.

He no longer spends the time to pick out a scent. This Christmas, my father handed me a gift card to a store famous for its perfumes and soaps, signed for the both of them in his new wife's cursive. No present says "I no longer know you" more than that.

I didn't see him this Father's Day. He went to a ballgame with his non-biological granddaughter. He's excellent with children. It's just hard to watch them grow up when he has spent the last fifty years staying the same age.

WRITTEN SOMETIME AFTER I LIVED IN YOU

When I was small, we were bandits.

I'd flutter-kick from the shopping cart
while she plucked grapes from the plastic
and popped them in my mouth.

So much laughter would spill
out of us, the grocery would announce
a cleanup in the produce aisle.

I remember when she cut my hair
with kitchen scissors, how she spent
the afternoon convincing me
I was still a girl.

Some days I envy the thermostat,
how she nurses its temperature
like a sneezing child's,
home sick from school.

Sometimes I resent the silverware,
still small enough to be bathed
by my mother in the kitchen sink.

THE YEAR SWING SET RUST
BEGAN TO TASTE LIKE BLOOD
from my mother's perspective

1.
The Bay Ridge of my childhood was a simple playground.
On the 69th Street Pier lucky fisherman would fillet
their catch, bones flying out of the red snapper's body
in chaos like children sent home early from school.

To hand-me-down Irish kids, an empty refrigerator
in a kitchen meant no dinner for the third night.
But an empty fridge in a neighbor's gutter
meant something else: a two-seater space rocket,
a submarine, the ultimate hiding spot.

At first Brooklyn played along, seeking
for the missing twins in Owl's Head Park,
in coat donation boxes of local churches,
beneath the skirts of barren women.

I don't remember the year it became law
to remove all refrigerator doors before disposal,
but I do remember the wake; the entire borough in black,
their mother trying to drown the remainder of the living world
with her sobs. Cold white coffins, like open toy chests, tempted every child
in the room fighting the want to unwrap them,
to awaken the perfectly still dolls. When we lowered
them into the ground, my mind made treasure maps, marking
where the city hid our Christmas presents.

2.
My babies are perfect: iced vanilla,
sprinkles of freckles, topped with tart cherry mouths.
Every mother dreams for children who sleep
like mine, immaculate as frozen pastries.
Sometimes in the night I'll scream
just to make certain
they'll stir.

Beginning in an Ice Cream Truck and Ending in a Court Room
after Kim Addonizio

When our breasts arrived
as a kind of currency, we'd tug
our camisoles low, use
our newfangled bodies to haggle
with the ice cream man. The winner
was the girl who received her chocolate cone
for free, who sucked on candy cigarettes
the same way she wore a training bra.
That summer my pockets grew forests
of hand-tied maraschino cherry stems:
tampered evidence that I might one day be worthy
of kissing. In exchange for rides
on the handlebars of their bikes,
we'd let the boys bite
the beads off our candy
necklaces until the chokers
resembled punched out teeth.
From their slobber, blue and violet dye
stained my throat where the sweetness
had once been. So I suppose,
Your Honor, I was preparing
for *him*.

THE FIRST TIME I MET HIS MOTHER, CHRISTMAS EVE

I offered to help carve the dinner beast,
which was how my meatless body knew
I really loved him.

She didn't need my help—
the adults would fix me
a cocktail in the backroom.

I met the usual characters: an aunt who cleaned up
the spill of her giggle with a paw over a lip-sticked mouth,
a cousin who smelled like a bar fight,
wedding ring tarnished as an ashtray.

I told his uncle that I liked his tie—
it had real Christmas lights sewn into it,
a ruby one for Rudolph's nose.
He suggested if I was so fond of that tie
we could pretend it was mistletoe,
his tarantula hand creeping toward my knee.

Oh, he's harmless his mother explained away,
*Just Uncle Lenny... a joke... In our family we can take
a joke* she informed, stringing a garland
of excuses for him being only a man.

From then on she looked at me like a gift
she wished came with a receipt, that her son would exchange
me for another—perhaps a doll with a smaller mouth,
soft legs that can't stand up for themselves,
a string in its back she could pull and unleash a fit
of mechanical laughter. *It was funny, a joke, harmless.*

THE LAST TIME I MET HIS MOTHER, VALENTINE'S DAY

She stood beside her son so proud,
like his date to an award ceremony,
as I waited for the judge to order five-hundred feet
between his cackle and my ear, his groin and my No,
his many sharp edges and my body
soft and scared as a dying lamb.
It was the first Valentine
I had ever given myself.

His mother sneered like I was a bitch
walking on her hind legs, an amusing stunt
with a false sense of spine. A little girl
making monsters out of molehills—
but she never needed my help.
She carved that beast herself.

SHOOT HER
after Jan Beatty

I forgive the writer who chiseled her name down to initials so she could sell more books—to boys. The fan girls who still bop along to that wife-beating musician, ignore the needle scratching the record like it's trying to draw blood. Forgive the nine college women who claimed not to be feminists on the first day of Women's Studies Class, the three who still weren't on the last. I am extracting my sharpest teeth, one by one. Forgive the sorority polluting the campus with flyers that read: "Don't be *that girl* who gets her drink roofied." Forgive them for the blame they'll save for their daughters, for the curfews they won't give their sons. Forgive the friend I confided in, told of his threats, who pleaded I harbor the details because she did not want to take sides—forgive her because in that moment she took his. The other who blamed my restraining order on PMS, an accusation that could set women back into whale-bone corsets. I am gnawing my nails down to the nubs. I forgive the skirted doctor who asked *is it considered rape if you'd already slept with him?* The gaggle of daughters whose smiles peel off their faces when I enter a room, who have turned my name into an insult, a warning, a synonym for pariah. I am wilting at the fist. Forgive those girls who are teaching me to not be *that girl*, that sometimes it's better to buy an eyelash curler and shut the fuck up. Forgive my mother for the yearlong eve of divorce, how we slept beside each other on air mattresses in the cellar, relinquished the entire upstairs to my father, forgive her for never showing me what it looks like to be in love. I forgive myself for how I marinated in hate for these women, how it made us the same. How I breastfed this anger like my only child. How I expected it to nurse me back. How I considered the gun before the white flag. How an olive branch almost became a bat. I am melting my brass knuckles down to tiny trumpets. I am singing this forgiveness song over and over, until I believe it.

The Runaways

We live in a nameless town. Our mailbox is red and rusted shut like a mouth that has not been kissed in fifty years. There is no mailman because there is no mail. These names have been borrowed from books we liked best. Beyond our wraparound porch there is nothing but infinite green. Throughout the day we fill an endless pitcher of half lemonade (Wendy's favorite) and half iced-tea (mine), and sway in our rocking chairs all afternoon watching the nothing pass by.

After all these years I'm still not much of a painter but that never stops me from painting. Wendy is not much of a singer but hers is my favorite voice. She picks the guitar as I play the strands of her hair, she hums, "*Alice, which note is that?*"

"*A-Flat,*" I answer.

When I paint it is always her dancing in the grass, her white dress drifting behind her like a less-skilled waltzer trying to keep time, but she moves with such whirlwind that I can never capture her face. Each canvas arrives as a blur, a layer of milk poured over a water lily. Wendy cries in C-Minor.

We know so much of each other's mouths that we no longer have to speak our fake names. Wendy can sense from the kitchen when my thoughts turn to what those men *did*, so she meets me by the tulips and seizes the gardening shears. When she trembles in the bathtub, I throw fistfuls of soothing lavender from the bush below her open window and they land on the bath mat. She does not say thank you and she does not need to. Instead, when I am cold under the stars she does not bring a spare afghan but shimmies her tiny body into my sleeping bag and we rest like two caterpillars tucked in the same cocoon.

The aroma of chocolate simmering in a saucepan alerts me that Wendy has gone to the place we never speak of. I know it's time to begin my part of the ritual. I build a piñata and she stuffs it with her freshly baked sweets as if packing the Trojan Horse with soldiers. She sews up its belly and I hand her the wooden bat but do not let go until her eyes meet mine. When I am certain she understands, I tie the blindfold, spin her around until she is drunk as a husband and let her swing. Striking tentatively at first, Wendy's beating crescendos as she slashes its body open and we dance in the candy rain.

I will never forget the day Wendy came to me, tools in hand, and we drilled holes through everything we once owned: engagement rings, baby's rattles, knocked-out teeth delivered by the hands of men who loved us so much we couldn't smile for anyone else. All that we have left has been turned to chimes—whose music plays loudest when the wind blows with fury, who sound most beautiful right after they've been struck.

THOMAS EDISON ON THE AMAZON RIVER

When light bulbs blew out, he was reminded
of his failure, his mockery of daylight.

Nightly, Thomas's lovers unscrewed
his invention, preferring the kindness
of candles.

He thought he'd been so clever, capturing the sun
in a mason jar, dreamed of it conveniently lighting
a porch scene while a girl rummaged
for her door key, or illuminating her face
as her sweetheart found her lips.

Instead it was the moths most drawn to his creation
and Thomas found himself responsible for the deaths
of a million naked butterflies.

In an effort to outrun his own name,
he built a raft, weaved his escape
beneath a pale ribbon of sky.

He drifted in the Amazon for a while,
admiring the work of a greater inventor:
His electric eels: votives of the sea,
the dimmer switch of the sun.

But when night fell,
Mr. Edison could not stop concocting:

Perhaps a cloak of sewn glowworms he mused,
should no one be able to find me?

*Or a bouillon cube of crushed fireflies for a soup
one can sip in the dark?*

*What if I could squeeze that bright flash of storm
into twin pendants for the ears of my darling, what then?
Would that not be the potion for love?*

Even in the quiet black of the river,
Thomas could dream
only of light.

THANKSGIVING DINNER
from my mother's perspective

So maybe I *did* smell the weed
slithering beneath my son's bedroom door
then tiptoeing down the staircase. Maybe I *knew*
it wasn't some suburban skunk—
but what was louder than that stink was the chorus
of laughter, my son *and* my daughter
getting along, finally sharing
something.

THE IRRATIONAL ANTHEM

We were down to the stale candy and pennies
at the bottom of the Halloween basket. Neighbors were moving
the skeletons from the front yard to the attic and the squirrels
were fat on faces we carved from pumpkins.
Spent two days trying to squeeze back into our human
costumes but you kept looking at me like I was still a Princess.

When we elected the new president, the streets
of our college town gushed with sound, car horns woo-hoo'd
and noisemakers hurrahed and above I could hear the sweet hallelujah
of liberals making love. If the world were to stop
for a minute, we could hear the confetti fall.
Love is quiet like that. I didn't know back then.

The other man arrived in limousines, charmed
desserts right onto our plates at restaurants where the placement
of silverware mattered. He laughed like a packed house encore
and could unzip my dress with only his eyes.
He made me feel like the only woman in the world.
He made a lot of women feel like that.

But you never picked up the bill. The only gift you ever gave
was a handmade binder of your father's poems, penned before
they laid him in the ground. I thought of the gold-leafed leather journal
the other man had given me, took notice of your book's tattered spine.
You did not teach me how to sneak a bill into a maître d's palm,
but how to stare at road kill until it became art.

I chose the man who knew the difference
between a Cabernet and Merlot by scent alone,
but still didn't know the color of my eyes.

Now you've moved to a new state with your apple pie woman
where the townsfolk speak in drawls, and the city girls
grow impatient at how your words fall like molasses
because you make sure you mean them before they leak out
your mouth.

But when your grandchildren ask where you were when the president
who looks most like your family won that night, you will remember
the pot smell of my apartment, the dizzying
tapestries, my stupid roommate who slept through
the changing world, how we celebrated with our skin
like two snapping firecrackers, how I begged you inside
my body and it was the most American thing we could do,
to pray like that.

The other man's love was a spectacle
of sound let loose in an empty room.
I spent years clawing after its echo.

That November was my last election.
I'll never step into another poll booth again.
Won't even allow myself the option of choosing
the wrong man.

25,498 Days Since I Last Saw You

Years later, did you look
for my name on the bookshelves?
Flip to the back cover to see if I'm still pretty,
how many kids I have, if
I mentioned you?

I am not what I once was.

My spine—curlicue and scoliosis
from crescent moons you bent into me.

Skin—sunset and jaundiced
from a daffodil you once rubbed
across my cheek.

Hair—silver as a daydream
of the cutlery we never owned.

In my rocking chair I recall our first kiss,
let a teacup put its mouth on me, try to fit
your name into the crossword puzzle.

Your wife knows you have dreamt
of making love to me again; in your sleep
you have broken both hips.

You tip with nickels, lint, and Lifesaver mints,
they are stale and brittle like staircase and bone.
The waitress wears *my* name on *her* tag. You repeat it
endlessly to the sugar packets. When you finally remember—
it will be like replacing the one faulty bulb
in a string of Christmas lights.

You'll bend a straw in Brooklyn,
my knuckle will crack on another continent.

I'll reach for dried apricots
and chew on your earlobes.

You'll coax dental floss from its plastic,
wedge my hair between your molars.

You will lose me one last time
in the sink drain.

When the doctors unlock my hospital gown,
it will be your hands unbuttoning my blouse,
the chill in the morgue—a long weekend snow day.

The autopsy is oblivious to how we lived.

A nurse drapes a sheet over my face,
I open my eyes to see you—young
and laughing in the bedclothes.

A Final Letter to His Writer Wife

Melinda,

I know that even if I drove until I hit water, even if one hundred women cast their tongues to fish your name from my mouth—we are never over. We are leather-bound in libraries. Years from now, grad students will dissect our stories as if invited to each private milestone; they'll know the secret name I called you, they'll know the words I whispered after our last attempt at a child exited you in a hotel toilet. In this way we'll live forever, like a shiny glass eye in a decaying corpse.

We don't meet *people* anymore, but potential characters. I know which women you will later shove into your typewriter if you ask them to speak of their fathers. I know the way you will portray the men by how they hold the necks of their beer bottles—if it's more caress or choke.

The saddest is when I undress you. You are not there. I kiss your neck and it seems you are pretending to be a viola. I pull a small shudder from within you—you are thinking of an exodus of swans. Your eyes dart around the room to swallow the surroundings the same way a typewriter slashes across a page. Sometimes there aren't swans, Melinda. Sometimes it's nothing but fucking in a car beneath the only blown-out streetlight because we're waiting to sober up before the drive home. It isn't always a poem. Sometimes it isn't lovemaking, but killing time.

So I'm leaving you now, and I know it won't be the worst thing I could do to you. You will find a way to thank me in an interview. The spine of your next book will be yanked from my back as I'm walking away. I know the worst thing I could do would be to come home every night with no perfume on my collar besides the scent of fucking the same woman for forty years, or I could help with the dishes and not throw them against the wall, or I could love you until your hair turned white and boring as a blank page. I am sure that even now, having anticipated this letter, you are typing manically of me, expecting the one who loves you most to constantly have his hand penning a note to leave you. Perhaps you are on a stage reading this very letter to strangers you hope will buy your book, or call you a bitch, or fuck you tonight and everyone will wonder if the letter is real, if I am real, and I won't know either. I won't know a goddamn thing what to tell them. Without you writing me into existence, am I even

FOR THOSE WHO ARE RIGHT NOW STILL LOOKING FOR CLOSURE:

Closure is a motherfucker.

Closure will tell you to meet it at the bus stop at 6:30, and you'll think Closure means 6:30 *that* day, but it really meant 6/30 as in June 30th, and didn't specify the year.

Perhaps you'll ask your ex to meet you at The Olive Garden and bring Closure with him, but he'll stupidly bring Closure's evil twin Openature and you'll be left wondering why Closure was being such a dick.

Maybe your best friend claims she found Closure in a dream once, and that's cool, but you've had dreams about your father where he's played by Eddie Murphy and at the time this makes perfect sense but when you wake up you're like "How'd I know that was my dad? My dad's a Jewish Dentist" and if Closure came to you in a dream would you even know what to look for?

By the process of elimination, I can't tell you where Closure *is*, but I know a few places where Closure is *not*:

1. On your ex-girlfriend's mother's answering machine.
2. Halfway through a bottle of Bacardi Grand Melon.
3. The bottom of the 59th Street Bridge.
4. In a box of Atomic Blue Hair Dye.
5. The chorus of Sinead O'Connor's "Nothing Compares 2 U."
6. Inside a stranger's body at midnight.
7. Inside that stranger's apartment at dawn.
8. In anything you can only buy from someone who still uses a beeper.

Closure could take seventy-six years to reach you, like Halley's comet. It might greet you by the airport check in, where your carry-on (filled with all the perfect comebacks to say *after* the fact, the roommate you lost over who would claim the bigger bedroom, the failed novels, the questions you never asked your father, every person you didn't say goodbye to) exceeds the weight limit. Suddenly Closure shows up, all polite-like, and offers to help check your bags. Just when you think you're going to accept you find yourself saying, "No. Keep them. Don't need any of *that* where I'm going. I'm leaving it behind."

GOD TALKS BACK

Megan,

I wish you'd stop prefacing your prayers
with "Dear." It's so formal, like a wax seal.
"Dear" makes me sound old. And I am…old.
But that doesn't make me any less hip, Megan.
I was listening to Bon Iver before you. I know bands
so underground they haven't left their basements yet.
But this isn't about that.

Now I suppose "Dear God" is better than "To Whom It May Concern,"
which is how your stockbroker friend Howard begins his prayers,
pleating his sterilized hands into a business fold.

"If you exist…" is also no way to open a prayer.
Imagine receiving a letter doubting that you were real.
This would compel you to prove your existence
in a really big way, like earthquakes, world wars
or poison ivy, and then they'd turn it all around
and use it as proof that you *definitely* do not exist.
It's the one game I cannot win.

As for the wishes—I tried. You begged
for Tommy Smith in kindergarten and when I delivered him
in tenth grade, Valentine in hand, you'd lost interest.
It was like saving up to buy your little girl a tricycle,
but by the time you present it to her she's ready to borrow your car.
When you're immortal, it's hard to remember
that humans don't have forever.
I'm sorry for the years I took my time.

You know I still remember your first prayer?
I keep it tucked behind my ear like a grandpa's magic penny.
You were six-years-old and crying for Bosnia,
a country so far away you could hardly pronounce it.
You pray selfishly now. That's okay.
I'd rather hear from you greedy than not at all.

Plus I know the old trick:
the kind who bookend their own wishes with "world peace!"
and "no hunger!" hoping I pick them first
from my giant grab bag of hope.
It's a lottery, really. I wish I could
say it was an exact science, a ticket called
at the deli counter, but it's not. Sometimes
you don't get chosen.

You were.
And you're welcome for returning
your brother. The drugs kept his finger on my doorbell.
I was tempted to keep him, even had a seat reserved in my choir,
but I could tell if he was taken from you,
you would have followed shortly after—
the way your cat Purry used to follow you
to school each morning.
(Purry is chillin', by the way.)
I could wait on your arrival, Megan.
You're a pain in the ass. A control freak, like me.
You'd be up here rearranging clouds, prioritizing the guest list
for The Upstairs Party, complaining of boredom.
You have plenty more to do down there
before we officially meet.

As for the prayers—seriously?
Asking me to make you skinny? Again?
You've been hounding me for this one since '97. I gave you working legs,
a ticking heart, a block to run around. Sure, I gave you cupcakes.
I also gave you the right to choose.

Regarding the boy, the one you returned
like a present you didn't feel you deserved,
the one with eyes so green they made you seasick—I do
let you see him again—in every dream thick with color, isn't that
       enough? No,
you won't always be alone. You won't only be naked in the shower, won't
have to teach yourself to kiss again on the back of your hand, and yes,
it's totally cool with me if you decide to like girls too.
Fucking awesome, in fact.

Do you remember The Game of Telephone?
How a chain of girls would pass around one whisper
and by the time it returned to you, your secret was no longer
your own? That's what working with messengers and missionaries
is like. Even now, this letter will arrive to you in all the wrong
dialects, its words sifted, but it's okay because I know you
heard me. Because the entire time you read this, these moments
I poured through you like sun floods a windowpane,
I was real.

THANK YOU

Mom, you have been so generous with your stories, your time and your exploding love. All my best magic spells I learned from you. Dad, your always-little girl just gave birth to her first book—this makes you a grandpa, congrats! Sean, you came back. I knew you would. You are the reason I became a writer—to tell of us. Panda, your face is still my inspiration and you will always be my roommate—our apartment is the universe. I have you and I have everything. Miles, your patience with this process is unmatched. You taught me what love *actually* means—the most hallelujah-worthy lesson of all. I will never be who I was before you again. Jeanann Verlee, Rachel McKibbens, and Mindy Nettifee, you braid together to be my second backbone. See how straight I'm standing? Tracy Soren and James Merenda, you are the family I chose—the family that chose me. Without all of you this book is impossible because without you *I* am impossible.

I also want to extend my unending gratitude to *Sip This* coffee house in Valley Stream, New York, for being so accommodating while I wrote this book there, for the many delicious soy vanilla dirty chai teas and necessary doses of caffeine. Mahogany L. Browne, Cristin O'Keefe Aptowicz, Ainsley Burrows, Mike McGee, Gypsee Yo, Mongo, Joanna Hoffman, Jon Sands and Andrea Gibson for all your encouragement in its many forms. Dennis Doherty, Jan Schmidt, and Larry Carr for being the best writing professors on this planet. The SUNY New Paltz Slam Team for being my roots and later appointing me their gardener. Write Bloody Publishing and Derrick Brown for cultivating this wild dream. To Josie, Gizmo, and Taco for keeping a girl smiling, warm, and sane. And you, for supporting the arts, for trusting me to the end, for building a better world. Love, unbound.

ACKNOWLEDGMENTS

Wholehearted thanks and recognition to the following publications where earlier versions of these poems first appeared:

Crescent City Review: "During the Week I Thought I Was Carrying Your Child"

Danse Macabre: "Boy Scout" and "The Pink Ribbon Parade"

Indiefeed Performance Poetry Podcast: "The Pink Ribbon Parade", "25,498 Days Since I Last Saw You", "Honest House" and "Boy Scout"

> *kill author*: "Penelope Pussycat Finally Speaks" and "Adam's Apple Pie"

The Legendary: "What the Hour Hand Said to the Minute Hand" and "We Had No Children"

Muzzle Magazine: "Beginning in an Ice Cream Truck and Ending in a Court Room"

The Nervous Breakdown: "Thomas Edison on the Amazon River"

PANK: "Friday Night Between 2nd Avenue and Herald Square", "Bringing Over the Jell-o Mold" and "The Atheist"

Static and Other Lungless Things Poetry Anthology (Penmanship Books 2009): "Pendulum"

Stonesthrow Review Anthology: "Written Sometime After I lived in You" and "25,498 Days Since I Last Saw You"

Union Station Magazine: "The Runaways"

Vinyl: "The Honest House"

About The Author

Megan Falley is a writer of poems, a lover of animals, and a dismantler of the patriarchy. She is a fierce poetry slam competitor and has represented New York City at the adult national level, and The State University of New York at New Paltz for four years on the collegiate circuit, a team she later returned to coach. In 2009, Megan co-founded the annual Wade-Lewis Poetry Slam Invitational, the second largest college poetry tournament in the country named after her late and beloved professor, which raises scholarship money for academically-driven students of color with substantial financial need. She is the recipient of the Tomaselli Award for Poetry, a prize granted to one graduating senior from New Paltz each year. After earning her degree in English Literature and Creative Writing in 2010, Falley honed her artistic focus to be a strong advocate for women and the abused. At age twenty-two, *After the Witch Hunt*, her first full-length collection, was accepted for publication. Her poetry has reached microphones as far as New Zealand, and hopefully, as close as your heart.

For more Megan, visit www.MeganFalley.com.

ABOUT THE BOOK

As if she discovered a small army of silenced women captive in her pen,
Megan Falley releases them in the spilled ink that is her first collection
of poems, *After the Witch Hunt*. Demanding "if you really love a writer,
bury her in all your awful and watch as she scrawls her way out," her
book does exactly that. An incessant digging, a journey in building
escape routes, armed with both humor and a brazen darkness, each
poem in this book of bloodletting is another swing of the pick and axe
in this young woman's labor, insistent upon light.

New Write Bloody Books for 2012

Strange Light
The *New York Times* says, "There's something that happens when you read Derrick Brown, a rekindling of faith in the weird, hilarious, shocking, beautiful power of words." This is the final collection from Derrick Brown, one of America's top-selling and touring poets. Everything hilarious and stirring is illuminated. The power of *Strange Light* is waiting.

Who Farted Wrong? Illustrated Weight Loss For the Mind
Syd Butler (of the sweet band, Les Savvy Fav) creates sketchy morsels to whet your appetite for wrong, and it will be delicious. There is no need to read between the lines of this new style of flash thinking speed illustration in this hilarious new book. Why? There are not that many lines.

New Shoes on a Dead Horse
The Romans believed that an artist's inspiration came from a spirit, called a genius, that lived in the walls of the artist's home. This character appears throughout Sierra DeMulder's book, providing charming commentary and biting insight on the young author's creative process and emotional path.

Good Grief
Elegantly-wrought misadventures as a freshly-graduated Michigan transplant, Stevie Edwards stumbles over foal legs through Chicago and kneels down to confront the wreckage of her skinned knees.

After the Witch Hunt
Megan Falley showcases her fresh, lucid poetry with a refreshing lack of jaded undertones. Armed with both humor and a brazen darkness, each poem in this book is another swing of the pick axe in this young woman's tunnel, insistent upon light.

I Love Science!
Humorous and thought provoking, Shanney Jean Maney's book effortlessly combines subjects that have previously been thought too diverse to have anything in common. Science, poetry and Jeff Goldblum form covalent bonds that put the poetic fire underneath our bunsen burners. A Lab Tech of words, Maney turns language into curious, knowledge-hungry poetry. Foreword by Lynda Barry.

Time Bomb Snooze Alarm
Bucky Sinister, a veteran poet of the working class, layers his gritty truths with street punk humor. A menagerie of strange people and stranger moments that linger in the dark hallway of Sinister's life. Foreword by Randy Blythe of "Lamb of God".

News Clips and Ego Trips
A collection of helpful articles from *Next...* magazine, which gave birth to the Southern California and national poetry scene in the mid-'90s. It covers the growth of spoken word, page poetry and slam, with interviews and profiles of many poets and literary giants like Patricia Smith, Henry Rollins and Miranda July. Edited by G. Murray Thomas.

Slow Dance With Sasquatch
Jeremy Radin invites you into his private ballroom for a waltz through the forest at the center of life, where loneliness and longing seamlessly shift into imagination and humor.

The Smell of Good Mud
Queer parenting in conservative Oklahoma, Lauren Zuniga finds humor and beauty in this collection of new poems. This explores the grit and splendor of collective living, and other radical choices. It is a field guide to blisters and curtsies.

OTHER WRITE BLOODY BOOKS (2003 - 2011)

Great Balls of Flowers (2009)
Steve Abee's poetry is accessible, insightful, hilarious, compelling,
upsetting, and inspiring. TNB Book of the Year.

Everything Is Everything (2010)
The latest collection from poet Cristin O'Keefe Aptowicz,
filled with crack squirrels, fat presidents, and el Chupacabra.

Working Class Represent (2011)
A young poet humorously balances an office job with the life
of a touring performance poet in Cristin O'Keefe Aptowicz's third book of poetry

Oh, Terrible Youth (2011)
Cristin O'Keefe Aptowicz's plump collection commiserates and celebrates
all the wonder, terror, banality and comedy that is the long journey to adulthood.

Hot Teen Slut (2011)
Cristin O'Keefe Aptowicz's second book recounts stories of
a virgin poet who spent a year writing for the porn business.

Dear Future Boyfriend (2011)
Cristin O'Keefe Aptowicz's debut collection of poetry tackles
love and heartbreak with no-nonsense honesty and wit.

38 Bar Blues (2011)
C. R. Avery's second book, loaded with bar-stool musicality and brass-knuckle poetry.

Catacomb Confetti (2010)
Inspired by nameless Parisian skulls in the catacombs of France,
Catacomb Confetti assures Joshua Boyd's poetic immortality.

Born in the Year of the Butterfly Knife (2004)
The Derrick Brown poetry collection that birthed Write Bloody Publishing.
Sincere, twisted, and violently romantic.

I Love You Is Back (2006)
A poetry collection by Derrick Brown.
"One moment tender, funny, or romantic, the next, visceral, ironic,
and revelatory—Here is the full chaos of life." (Janet Fitch, *White Oleander*)

Scandalabra (2009)
Former paratrooper Derrick Brown releases a stunning collection of poems written
at sea and in Nashville, TN. About.com's book of the year for poetry.

Workin' Mime to Five (2011)
Dick Richards is a fired cruise ship pantomimist. You too can learn
his secret, creative pantomime moves. Humor by Derrick Brown.

Don't Smell the Floss (2009)
Award-winning writer Matty Byloos' first book of bizarre, absurd, and deliciously
perverse short stories puts your drunk uncle to shame.

Reasons to Leave the Slaughter (2011)
Ben Clark's book of poetry revels in youthful discovery from the heartland
and the balance between beauty and brutality.

Birthday Girl with Possum (2011)
Brendan Constantine's second book of poetry examines the invisible lines
between wonder & disappointment, ecstasy & crime, savagery & innocence.

The Bones Below (2010)
National Slam Champion Sierra DeMulder performs and teaches
with the release of her first book of hard-hitting, haunting poetry.

The Constant Velocity of Trains (2008)
The brain's left and right hemispheres collide in Lea Deschenes' Pushcart-Nominated
book of poetry about physics, relationships, and life's balancing acts.

Heavy Lead Birdsong (2008)
Award-winning academic poet Ryler Dustin releases his most
definitive collection of surreal love poetry.

Uncontrolled Experiments in Freedom (2008)
Boston underground art scene fixture Brian Ellis
becomes one of America's foremost narrative poetry performers.

Yesterday Won't Goodbye (2011)
Boston gutter punk Brian Ellis releases his second book of poetry,
filled with unbridled energy and vitality.

Write About an Empty Birdcage (2011)
Debut collection of poetry from Elaina M. Ellis that flirts with loss,
reveres appetite, and unzips identity.

Ceremony for the Choking Ghost (2010)
Slam legend Karen Finneyfrock's second book of poems ventures
into the humor and madness that surrounds familial loss.

Pole Dancing to Gospel Hymns (2008)
Andrea Gibson, a queer, award-winning poet who tours with Ani DiFranco,
releases a book of haunting, bold, nothing-but-the-truth ma'am poetry.

These Are the Breaks (2011)
Essays from one of hip-hops deftest public intellectuals, Idris Goodwin

Bring Down the Chandeliers (2011)
Tara Hardy, a working-class queer survivor of incest, turns sex,
trauma and forgiveness inside out in this collection of new poems.

City of Insomnia (2008)
Victor D. Infante's noir-like exploration of unsentimental truth and poetic exorcism.

The Last Time as We Are (2009)
A new collection of poems from Taylor Mali, the author
of "What Teachers Make," the most forwarded poem in the world.

In Search of Midnight: the Mike Mcgee Handbook of Awesome (2009)
Slam's geek champion/class clown Mike McGee on his search for midnight
through hilarious prose, poetry, anecdotes, and how-to lists.

1,000 Black Umbrellas (2011)
Daniel McGinn's first internationally released collection from 'everyone's favorite
unknown author' sings from the guts with the old school power of poetry.

Over the Anvil We Stretch (2008)
2-time poetry slam champ Anis Mojgani's first collection: a Pushcart-Nominated
batch of backwood poetics, Southern myth, and rich imagery.

The Feather Room (2011)
Anis Mojgani's second collection of poetry explores storytelling and
poetic form while traveling farther down the path of magic realism.

Animal Ballistics (2009)
Trading addiction and grief for empowerment and humor with her poetry,
Sarah Morgan does it best.

Rise of the Trust Fall (2010)
Award-winning feminist poet Mindy Nettifee
releases her second book of funny, daring, gorgeous, accessible poems.

Love in a Time of Robot Apocalypse (2011)
Latino-American poet David Perez releases his first book
of incisive, arresting, and end-of-the-world-as-we-know-it poetry.

No More Poems About the Moon (2008)
A pixilated, poetic and joyful view of a hyper-sexualized,
wholeheartedly confused, weird, and wild America with Michael Roberts.

The New Clean (2011)
Jon Sands' poetry redefines what it means to laugh, cry, mop it up and start again.

Miles of Hallelujah (2010)
Slam poet/pop-culture enthusiast Rob "Ratpack Slim" Sturma
shows first collection of quirky, fantastic, romantic poetry.

Sunset at the Temple of Olives (2011)
Paul Suntup's unforgettable voice merges subversive surrealism
and vivid grief in this debut collection of poetry.

Spiking the Sucker Punch (2009)
Nerd heartthrob, award-winning artist and performance poet,
Robbie Q. Telfer stabs your sensitive parts with his wit-dagger.

Racing Hummingbirds (2010)
Poet/performer Jeanann Verlee releases an award-winning book
of expertly crafted, startlingly honest, skin-kicking poems.

Live for a Living (2007)
Acclaimed performance poet Buddy Wakefield releases his second collection
about healing and charging into life face first.

Gentleman Practice (2011)
Righteous Babe Records artist and 3-time International Poetry Champ
Buddy Wakefield spins a nonfiction tale of a relay race to the light.

How to Seduce a White Boy in Ten Easy Steps (2011)
Debut collection for feminist, biracial poet Laura Yes Yes
dazzles with its explorations into the politics and metaphysics of identity.

WRITE BLOODY ANTHOLOGIES

The Elephant Engine High Dive Revival (2009)
Our largest tour anthology ever! Features unpublished work by
Buddy Wakefield, Derrick Brown, Anis Mojgani and Shira Erlichman!

The Good Things About America (2009)
American poets team up with illustrators to recognize the beauty and wonder in our
nation. Various authors. Edited by Kevin Staniec and Derrick Brown

Junkyard Ghost Revival (2008)
Tour anthology of poets, teaming up for a journey of the US in a small van.
Heart-charging, socially active verse.

The Last American Valentine:
Illustrated Poems To Seduce And Destroy (2008)
Acclaimed authors including Jack Hirschman, Beau Sia, Jeffrey McDaniel,
Michael McClure, Mindy Nettifee and more. 24 authors and 12 illustrators
team up for a collection of non-sappy love poetry. Edited by Derrick Brown

Learn Then Burn (2010)
Exciting classroom-ready anthology for introducing new writers
to the powerful world of poetry. Edited by Tim Stafford and Derrick Brown.

Learn Then Burn Teacher's Manual (2010)
Tim Stafford and Molly Meacham's turn key classroom-safe guide
to accompany *Learn Then Burn*: A modern poetry anthology for the classroom.

Knocking at the Door: Poems for Approaching the Other (2011)
An exciting compilation of diverse authors that explores the concept of the Other
from all angles. Innovative writing from emerging and established poets.

WRITEBLOODY
QUALITY AMERICAN WRITING

WWW.WRITEBLOODY.COM

Pull Your Books Up
By Their Bootstraps

Write Bloody Publishing distributes and promotes great books of fiction, poetry and art every year. We are an independent press dedicated to quality literature and book design, with an office in Long Beach, CA.

Our employees are authors and artists so we call ourselves a family. Our design team comes from all over America: modern painters, photographers and rock album designers create book covers we're proud to be judged by.

We publish and promote 8-12 tour-savvy authors per year. We are grass-roots, D.I.Y., bootstrap believers. Pull up a good book and join the family. Support independent authors, artists and presses.

Visit us online:

WRITEBLOODY.COM

CPSIA information can be obtained
at www.ICGtesting.com
Printed in the USA
FFOW02n1835220316
22508FF

9 781935 904625